Orthodox Theological Texts

THE ORTHODOX VENERATION OF
MARY THE BIRTHGIVER OF GOD

The veneration of the Mother of God. 14th-century fresco from
the Church of St. Clement in Ochrid, Serbia.

The Orthodox Veneration of

MARY

The Birthgiver of God

by St. John Maximovitch

Translated, with an Introduction
by Fr. Seraphim Rose

*New edition to commemorate the
canonization of St. John Maximovitch*

ST. HERMAN OF ALASKA BROTHERHOOD
1996

Originally published under the title:
"The Orthodox Veneration of the Mother of God"
by Archbishop John Maximovitch.

Translated from the Orthodox Calendar for 1933
of the St. Job Brotherhood, Vladimirova,
Czechoslovakia.

Address all correspondence to:
St. Herman of Alaska Brotherhood
P.O. Box 70
Platina, California 96076

Front cover: Icon of the Mother of God by Pimen Maximovitch Sofronov.

Library of Congress Cataloging in Publication Data

Maximovitch, St. John (1896-1966)
The Orthodox veneration of Mary the Birthgiver of God.
Translated from the Russian.

Library of Congress Catalog Number: 94-066189
ISBN: 0-938635-68-9

PREFACE
to the Fourth Edition

THIS NEW EDITION of the now-canonized St. John Maximovitch's treatise on Mary the Birthgiver of God, translated by Fr. Seraphim Rose, is coming out with the hope that it will inspire English-speaking readers to go deeper into the active veneration of the Mother of God, who is capable of helping the poor Christian race as it faces today an unprecedented state of confusion. The origin of this confusion is, of course, the Evil One. But the reason why the confusion is so intense today is because Orthodox Christians are rapidly losing love for Truth, and this automatically evokes fear in them before the powerful of this world. Love for Truth is the cornerstone of spiritual life as well as an assurance of our spiritual survival when the society's conscience has joined forces with the spirit of this world.

St. John Maximovitch was persecuted during his lifetime, even unto being placed in a secular court as a criminal, precisely because of his uncompromising adherence to the Truth. His writings have become Patristic texts of the modern age, for they have the same tone as those of the ancient Holy Fathers. It was this timeless quality in them that attracted the late Fr. Seraphim to translate them and make them available to contemporary Orthodox Christians.

The cover icon of the Mother of God was painted by the renowned iconographer Pimen M. Sofronov, as commissioned by Archbishop John Maximovitch. It was the main icon in the iconostasis of Archbishop John's Cathedral, where he served Liturgy up until his death in 1966. A few years after Archbishop John died, the icon was given to the St. Herman of Alaska Monastery church, where it was placed in the iconostasis before which both the ordination and the funeral of Fr. Seraphim took place.

We remember well how Archbishop John prayed before this icon and often stood beside it while delivering sermons during the last few years of his life on earth. Thus it is a fitting memorial both to the author of this work, St. John Maximovitch, and to the translator-publisher, Fr. Seraphim, that we present this new edition with the hope that Orthodox Christians will increase their prayers to the Mother of God.

In this new edition, we have included the main Akathist to the Mother of God, translated into English by another venerator of St. John Maximovitch, a man who also labored much to disseminate Orthodoxy to the English-speaking world—the late Archimandrite Lazarus Moore.

Abbot Herman
St. Paisius Abbey

CONTENTS

The original Iveron Icon of the Mother of God, with riza,
in the Iveron Monastery on Mount Athos, Greece.

INTRODUCTION

The Orthodox Theology of Archbishop John Maximovitch

BY FR. SERAPHIM ROSE OF PLATINA

NOT TOO MANY years ago the Abbess of a convent of the Russian Orthodox Church, a woman of righteous life, was delivering a sermon in the convent church on the feast of the Dormition of the Most Holy Mother of God. With tears she entreated her nuns and the pilgrims who had come for the feast to accept entirely and wholeheartedly what the Church hands down to us, taking such pains to preserve this tradition sacredly all these centuries—and not to choose for oneself what is "important" and what is "dispensable"; for by thinking oneself wiser than the tradition, one may end by losing the tradition. Thus, when the Church tells us in her hymns and icons that the Apostles were miraculously gathered from the ends of the earth in order to be present at the repose and burial of the Mother of God, we as Orthodox Christians are not free to deny this or reinterpret it, but must believe as the Church hands it down to us, with simplicity of heart.

A young Western convert who had learned Russian was present when this sermon was delivered. He himself had thought about this very subject, having seen icons in the traditional iconographic style depicting the Apostles being trans-

ported on clouds to behold the Dormition of the Theotokos;*
and he had asked himself the question: are we actually to
understand this "literally," as a miraculous event, or is it only a
"poetic" way of expressing the coming together of the Apostles
for this event ... or perhaps even an imaginative or "ideal"
depiction of an event that never occurred in fact? (Such, indeed,
are some of the questions with which "Orthodox theologians"
occupy themselves in our days.) The words of the righteous
Abbess therefore struck him to the heart, and he understood
that there was something deeper to the reception and understanding of Orthodoxy than what our own mind and feelings
tell us. In that instant the tradition was being handed down to
him, not from books but from a living vessel which contained
it; and it had to be received, not with mind or feelings only, but
above all with the heart, which in this way began to receive its
deeper training in Orthodoxy.

Later this young convert encountered, in person or through
reading, many people who were learned in Orthodox theology.
They were the "theologians" of our day, those who had been to
Orthodox schools and become theological "experts." They were
usually quite eager to speak on what was Orthodox and what
non-Orthodox, what was important and what secondary in
Orthodoxy itself; and a number of them prided themselves on
being "conservatives" or "traditionalists" in faith. But in none
of them did he sense the authority of the simple Abbess who
had spoken to his heart, unlearned as she was in such "theology."

And the heart of this convert, still taking his baby steps in
Orthodoxy, longed to know *how to believe,* which means also
whom to believe. He was too much a person of his times and his
own upbringing to be able simply to deny his own reasoning
power and believe blindly everything he was told; and it is very

---

* *Theotokos:* Greek for "God-birthgiver."

evident that Orthodoxy does not at all demand this of one—the very writings of the Holy Fathers are a living memorial of the working of human reason enlightened by the grace of God. But it was also obvious that there was something very much lacking in the "theologians" of our day, who for all their logic and their knowledge of Patristic texts, did not convey the feeling or savor of Orthodoxy as well as a simple, theologically-uneducated Abbess.

Our convert found the end of his search—the search for contact with the true and living tradition of Orthodoxy—in Archbishop John Maximovitch. For here he found someone who was a learned theologian in the "old" school and at the same time was very much aware of all the criticisms of that theology which have been made by the theological critics of our century, and was able to use his keen intelligence to find the truth where it might be disputed. But he also possessed something which none of the wise "theologians" of our time seem to possess: the same simplicity and authority which the pious Abbess had conveyed to the heart of the young God-seeker. His heart and mind were won: not because Archbishop John became for him an "infallible expert"—for the Church of Christ does not know any such thing—but because he saw in this holy archpastor a model of Orthodoxy, a true theologian whose theology proceeded from a holy life and from total rootedness in Orthodox tradition. When he spoke, his words could be trusted—although he carefully distinguished between the Church's teaching, which is certain, and his own personal opinions, which might be mistaken, and he bound no one to the latter. And our young convert discovered that, for all of Archbishop John's intellectual keenness and critical ability, his words much more often agreed with those of the simple Abbess than with those of the learned theologians of our time.

THE THEOLOGICAL WRITINGS of Archbishop John belong to no distinctive "school," and they do not reveal the extraordinary "influence" of any theologians of the recent past. It is true that Archbishop John was inspired to theologize, as well as to become a monk and enter the Church's service, by his great teacher, Metropolitan Anthony Khrapovitsky; and it is also true that the student made his own the teacher's emphasis on a "return to the Fathers" and to a theology closely bound to spiritual and moral life rather than academic. But Metropolitan Anthony's own theological writings are quite different in tone, intention, and content: he was very much involved with the theological academic world and with the intelligentsia of his time, and much of his writing is devoted to arguments and apologies which will be understandable to these elements of the society he knew. The writings of Archbishop John, on the other hand, are quite devoid of this apologetic and disputatious aspect. He did not *argue,* he simply presented the Orthodox teaching; and when it was necessary to refute false doctrines, as especially in his two long articles on the Sophiology of Bulgakov, his words were convincing not by virtue of logical argumentation, but rather by the power of his presentation of the Patristic teaching in its original texts. He did not speak to the academic or learned world, but to the uncorrupted Orthodox conscience; and he did not speak of a "return to the Fathers," because what he himself wrote was simply a handing down of the Patristic tradition, with no attempt to apologize for it.

The sources of Archbishop John's theology are, quite simply: Holy Scripture, the Holy Fathers (especially the great Fathers of the 4th and 5th centuries), and—most distinctively—the Divine services of the Orthodox Church. The latter source, rarely used to such an extent by the theologians of recent centuries, gives us a clue to the practical, un-academic approach of Archbishop John to theology. It is obvious that he was thoroughly immersed in the Church's Divine services and that his theological inspiration came chiefly from this primary Patristic source which he imbibed, not in leisure hours set apart for theologizing, but in his daily practice of *being present at every Divine service.* He drank in theology as an integral part of daily life, and it was doubtless this more than his formal theological studies that actually made him a theologian.

It is understandable, therefore, that one will not find in Archbishop John any theological "system." To be sure, he did not protest against the great works of "systematic theology" which the 19th century produced in Russia, and he made free use in his missionary work of the systematic catechisms of this period (as, in general, the great hierarchs of the 19th and 20th centuries have done, both in Greece and Russia, seeing in these catechisms an excellent aid to the work of Orthodox enlightenment among the people); in this respect he was above the fashions and parties of theologians and students, both past and present, who are a little too attached to the particular way in which Orthodox theology is presented. He showed equal respect for Metropolitan Anthony Khrapovitsky with his "anti-Western" emphasis, and for Metropolitan Peter Mogila with his supposedly excessive "Western influence." When the defects of one or the other of these great hierarchs and defenders of Orthodoxy would be presented to him, he would make a deprecating gesture with his hand and say, "unimportant"—because he always had in view first of all the great Patristic tradition which these theologians were successfully handing down in spite of their faults. In this respect he has much to teach the younger theologians of our own day, who approach Orthodox theology in a spirit that is often both too theoretical and too polemical and partisan.

For Archbishop John the theological "categories" of even the wisest of theological scholars were also "unimportant"—or rather, they were important only to the extent that they communicated a real meaning and did not become merely a matter of rote learning. One incident from his Shanghai years vividly reveals the freedom of his theological spirit: Once when he was attending the oral examinations of the senior catechism class of his cathedral school, he interrupted the perfectly correct recitation by one pupil of the list of Minor Prophets of the Old Testament with the abrupt and categorical assertion: *"There are no minor prophets!"* The priest-teacher of this class was understandably offended at this seeming disparagement of his teaching authority, but probably to this day the students remember this strange disruption of the normal catechism "categories," and possibly a few of them understood the message which Archbishop John tried to convey: with God *all* prophets are great, are "major," and this fact is more important than all the categories of our knowledge of them, however valid these are in themselves. In his theological writings and sermons also, Archbishop John often gives a surprising turn to his discourse which uncovers for us some unexpected aspect or deeper meaning of the subject he is discussing. It is obvious that for him theology is no mere human, earthly discipline whose riches are exhausted by our rational interpretations, or at which we can become self-satisfied "experts,"—but rather something that points heavenward and should draw our minds to God and heavenly realities, which are not grasped by logical systems of thought.

One noted Russian Church historian, N. Talberg, has suggested (in the *Chronicle* of Bishop Savva, ch. 23) that Archbishop John is to be understood first of all as "a fool for Christ's sake who remained such even in episcopal rank," and in this respect he compares him to St. Gregory the Theologian, who also did not conform, in ways similar to Archbishop John, to the standard "image" of a bishop. It is this "foolishness" (by the world's standards) that gives a characteristic tone to the theological writings both of St. Gregory and of Archbishop John: a certain detachment from public opinion, what "everyone thinks" and thus the belonging to no "party" or "school"; the approach to theological questions from an exalted, non-academic point of view and thus the healthy avoidance of petty disputes and the quarrelsome spirit; the fresh, unexpected turns of thought which make their theological writings first of all a source of inspiration and of a truly deeper understanding of God's revelation.

Perhaps most of all one is impressed by the utter *simplicity* of Archbishop John's writings. It is obvious that he accepts the Orthodox tradition straightforwardly and entirely, with no "double" thoughts as to how one can believe the tradition and still be a "sophisticated" modern man. He was aware of modern "criticism," and if asked could give his sound reasons for not accepting it on most points. He studied thoroughly the question of "Western influence" in Orthodoxy in recent centuries and had a well-balanced view of it, carefully distinguishing between what is to be rejected outright as foreign to Orthodoxy, what is to be discouraged but without "making an issue" over it, and what is to be accepted as conducive to true Orthodox life and piety (a point that is especially revealing of Archbishop John's lack of "preconceived opinions," and his testing of everything by sound Orthodoxy). But despite all his knowledge and exercise of critical judgment, he continued to believe the Orthodox tradition simply, just as the Church has handed it down to us. Most Orthodox theologians of our time, even if they may have escaped the worst effects of the Protestant-reformer mentality, still view Orthodox tradition through the spectacles of the academic environment in which they are at home; but Archbishop John was "at home" first and foremost in the church services at which he spent many hours every day, and thus the tinge of rationalism (not necessarily in a bad sense) of even the best of academic theologians was totally absent in his thought. In his writings there are no "problems"; his usually numerous footnotes are solely for the sake of informing where the teaching of the Church is to be found. In this respect he is absolutely at one with the "mind of the Fathers," and he appears in our midst as one of them, and not as a mere commentator on the theology of the past.

The theological writings of Archbishop John, printed in various church periodicals over four decades, have not yet been collected in one place. Those presently available to the St. Herman of Alaska Brotherhood would fill a volume of something more than 200 pages. His longer writings belong for the most part to his earlier years as a hieromonk in Yugoslavia, where he was already noted as outstanding among Orthodox theologians. Especially valuable are his two articles on the Sophiology of Bulgakov, one of them revealing convincingly, in a very objective manner, Bulgakov's total incompetence as a Patristic scholar, and the other being of even greater value as a classic exposition of the true Patristic doctrine of the Divine Wisdom. Among his later writings one should mention his article on Orthodox iconography (where, incidentally, he shows himself much more aware than his teacher, Metr. Anthony, of the question of "Western influence" in iconographic style); the series of sermons entitled "Three Evangelical Feasts," where he uncovers the deeper meaning of some of the "lesser" church feasts; and the article "The Church: the Body of Christ." His short articles and sermons also are deeply theological. One sermon begins with a "Hymn to God" of St. Gregory the Theologian and continues, in the same exalted, Patristic tone, as an inspired accusation against contemporary godlessness; another, spoken on Passion Friday, 1936, is a moving address to Christ lying in the tomb, in a tone worthy of the same Holy Father.

Archbishop John as a hieromonk in 1927,
at the time he was writing the present work.

We begin this series of translations with Archbishop John's classic exposition of the Orthodox veneration of the Mother of God and of the chief errors which have attacked it. Its longest chapter is a clear and striking refutation of the Latin dogma of the "Immaculate Conception."

Tolga Icon of the Theotokos ("God-Birthgiver"), from the Tolga
Monastery in Russia, where the relics of St. Ignatius
Brianchaninov are treasured.

I

The Veneration of the Mother of God During Her Earthly Life

FROM APOSTOLIC TIMES and to our days all who truly love Christ give veneration to Her Who gave birth to Him, raised Him and protected Him in the days of His youth. If God the Father chose Her, God the Holy Spirit descended upon Her, and God the Son dwelt in Her, submitted to Her in the days of His youth, was concerned for Her when hanging on the Cross—then should not everyone who confesses the Holy Trinity venerate Her?

Still in the days of Her earthly life the friends of Christ, the Apostles, manifested a great concern and devotion for the Mother of the Lord, especially the Evangelist John the Theologian, who, fulfilling the will of Her Divine Son, took Her to himself and took care for Her as for a mother from the time when the Lord uttered to him from the Cross the words: "Behold thy mother."

The Evangelist Luke painted a number of images of Her, some together with the Pre-eternal Child, others without Him. When he brought them and showed them to the Most Holy Virgin, She approved them and said: "The grace of My Son shall be with them," and repeated the hymn She had once sung in

St. John Damascene's Icon of the Theotokos "Of the Three Hands" in Hilandar Serbian Monastery on Mount Athos.

the house of Elizabeth: "My soul doth magnify the Lord, and My spirit hath rejoiced in God My Saviour."

However, the Virgin Mary during Her earthly life avoided the glory which belonged to Her as the Mother of the Lord. She preferred to live in quiet and prepare Herself for the departure into eternal life. To the last day of Her earthly life She took care to prove worthy of the Kingdom of Her Son, and before death She prayed that He might deliver Her soul from the malicious spirits that meet human souls on the way to heaven and strive to seize them so as to take them away with them to hades. The Lord fulfilled the prayer of His Mother and in the hour of Her death Himself came from heaven with a multitude of angels to receive Her soul.

Since the Mother of God had also prayed that She might bid farewell to the Apostles, the Lord gathered for Her death all the Apostles, except Thomas, and they were brought by an invisible power on that day to Jerusalem from all the ends of the inhabited world, where they were preaching, and they were present at Her blessed translation into eternal life.

The Apostles gave Her most pure body over to burial with sacred hymns, and on the third day they opened the tomb so as once more to venerate the remains of the Mother of God together with the Apostle Thomas, who had arrived then in Jerusalem. But they did not find the body in the tomb and in perplexity they returned to their own place; and then, during their meal, the Mother of God Herself appeared to them in the air, shining with heavenly light, and informed them that Her Son had glorified Her body also, and She, resurrected, stood before His Throne. At the same time, She promised to be with them always.

The Apostles greeted the Mother of God with great joy and began to venerate Her not only as the Mother of their beloved Teacher and Lord, but also as their heavenly helper, as a protector of Christians and intercessor for the whole human race before the Righteous Judge. And everywhere the Gospel of Christ was preached, His Most Pure Mother also began to be glorified.

The original Vladimir Icon of the Theotokos from the
Dormition Cathedral in Moscow, now treasured in
Moscow's Tretiakov Gallery.

II

The First Enemies of the Veneration of The Mother of God

THE MORE the faith of Christ spread and the Name of the Saviour of the world was glorified on earth, and together with Him also She Who was vouchsafed to be the Mother of the God-Man,—the more did the hatred of the enemies of Christ increase towards Her. Mary was the Mother of Jesus. She manifested a hitherto unheard-of example of purity and righteousness, and furthermore, now departed from this life, She was a mighty support for Christians, even though invisible to bodily eyes. Therefore all who hated Jesus Christ and did not believe in Him, who did not understand His teaching, or to be more precise, did not wish to understand as the Church understood, who wished to replace the preaching of Christ with their own human reasonings—all of these transferred their hatred for Christ, for the Gospel and the Church, to the Most Pure Virgin Mary. They wished to belittle the Mother, so as thereby to destroy faith also in Her Son, to create a false picture of Her among men in order to have the opportunity to rebuild the whole Christian teaching on a different foundation. In the womb of Mary, God and man were joined. She was the One Who served as it were as the ladder for the Son of God, Who descended from heaven. To strike a blow at Her veneration means to strike Christianity at the root, to destroy it in its very foundation.

And the very beginning of Her heavenly glory was marked on earth by an outburst of malice and hatred toward Her by unbelievers. When, after Her holy repose, the Apostles were carrying Her body for burial in Gethsemane, to the place chosen by her, John the Theologian went ahead carrying the branch from paradise which the Archangel Gabriel had brought to the Holy Virgin three days before this when he came from heaven to announce to Her Her approaching departure to the heavenly mansions.

"When Israel went out of Egypt, and the house of Jacob from among a barbarous people," chanted St. Peter from Psalm 113; "Alleluia," sang the whole assembly of the Apostles together with their disciples, as for example, Dionysius the Areopagite, who likewise had been miraculously transported at that time to Jerusalem. And while this sacred hymn was being sung, which was called by the Jews the "Great Alleluia," that is, the great "Praise ye the Lord," one Jewish priest, Athonius, leaped up to the bier and wished to overturn it and throw to the ground the body of the Mother of God.

The brazenness of Athonius was immediately punished: the Archangel Michael with an invisible sword cut off his hand, which remained hanging on the bier. The thunderstruck Athonius, experiencing a tormenting pain, in awareness of his sin, turned in prayer to the Jesus Whom he had hated up to then and he was immediately healed. He did not delay in accepting Christianity and confessing it before his former co-religionists, for which he received from them a martyr's death. Thus, the attempt to offend the honor of the Mother of God served for Her greater glorification.

The enemies of Christ resolved not to manifest their lack of veneration for the body of the Most Pure One further at that time by crude violence, but their malice did not cease. Seeing that Christianity was spreading everywhere, they began to spread various vile slanders about Christians. They did not spare the name of the Mother of Christ either, and they invented the story that Jesus of Nazareth had come from a base and immoral environment, and that His Mother had associated with a certain Roman soldier.

But here the lie was too evident for this fiction to attract serious attention. The whole family of Joseph the Betrothed and Mary Herself were known well by the inhabitants of Nazareth and the surrounding countryside in their time. *Whence hath this man this wisdom and these mighty works? Is not this the carpenter's son? Is not his mother called Mary, and his brethren: James and Joseph and Simon and Judas? And his sisters, are they not all with us?* (Matt. 13:54-55; Mark 6:3; Luke 4:22.) So said His fellow-countrymen in Nazareth when Christ revealed before them in the synagogue His other-worldly wisdom. In small towns the family matters of everyone are well known; very strict watch was kept then over the purity of married life.

Would people really have behaved with respect towards Jesus, called Him to preach in the synagogue, if He had been born of illegitimate cohabitation? To Mary the law of Moses would have been applied, which commanded that such persons be stoned to death; and the Pharisees would have taken the opportunity many times to reproach Christ for the conduct of His Mother. But just the contrary was the case. Mary enjoyed great respect; at Cana She was an honored guest at the wedding, and even when Her Son was condemned, no one allowed himself to ridicule or censure His Mother.

The Dormition of the Theotokos, showing the punishment of
the blasphemer Athonius. Fresco of 1295 in the Church of
St. Clement in Ochrid, Serbia.

III

Attempts of Jews and Heretics to Dishonor The Ever-Virginity of Mary

THE JEWISH slanderers soon became convinced that it was almost impossible to dishonor the Mother of Jesus, and on the basis of the information which they themselves possessed it was much easier to prove Her praiseworthy life. Therefore, they abandoned this slander of theirs, which had already been taken up by the pagans (Origen, *Against Celsus, I*), and strove to prove at least that Mary was not a virgin when She gave birth to Christ. They even said that the prophecies concerning the birth-giving of the Messiah by a virgin had never existed, and that therefore it was entirely in vain that Christians thought to exalt Jesus by the fact that a prophecy was supposedly being fulfilled in Him.

Jewish translators were found (Aquila, Symmachus, Theodotion) who made new translations of the Old Testament into Greek and in these translated the well-known prophecy of Isaiah (Is. 7:14) thus: *Behold, a young woman will conceive.* They asserted that the Hebrew word *Aalma* signified "young woman" and not "virgin," as stood in the sacred translation of the Seventy Translators [Septuagint], where this passage had been translated "Behold, a virgin shall conceive."

By this new translation they wished to prove that Christians, on the basis of an incorrect translation of the word *Aalma*, thought to ascribe to Mary something completely impossible—

a birth-giving without a man, while in actuality the birth of Christ was not in the least different from other human births.

However, the evil intention of the new translators was clearly revealed because by a comparison of various passages in the Bible it became clear that the word *Aalma* signified precisely "virgin." And indeed, not only the Jews, but even the pagans, on the basis of their own traditions and various prophecies, expected the Redeemer of the world to be born of a Virgin. The Gospels clearly stated that the Lord Jesus had been born of a Virgin.

How shall this be, seeing I know not a man? asked Mary, Who had given a vow of virginity, of the Archangel Gabriel, who had informed Her of the birth of Christ.

And the Angel replied: *The Holy Spirit shall come upon Thee, and the power of the Most High shall overshadow Thee; wherefore also that which is to be born shall be holy, and shall be called the Son of God* (Luke 1:34-35).

Later the Angel appeared also to righteous Joseph, who had wished to put away Mary from his house, seeing that She had conceived without entering into conjugal cohabitation with him. To Joseph the Archangel Gabriel said: *Fear not to take unto thee Mary thy wife: for that which is begotten in Her is of the Holy Spirit,* and he reminded him of the prophecy of Isaiah that a virgin would conceive (Matt. 1:18-25).

The rod of Aaron that budded, the rock torn away from the mountain without hands, seen by Nebuchadnezzar in a dream and interpreted by the Prophet Daniel, the closed gate seen by the Prophet Ezekiel, and much else in the Old Testament, prefigured the birth-giving of the Virgin. Just as Adam had been created by the Word of God from the unworked and virgin earth, so also the Word of God created flesh for Himself from a virgin womb when the Son of God became the new Adam so

The original Kursk Icon of the Theotokos,
once in the Kursk Monastery in Russia,
and now in New York City.

as to correct the fall into sin of the first Adam (St. Irenaeus of Lyons, Book III).

The seedless birth of Christ can and could be denied only by those who deny the Gospel, whereas the Church of Christ from of old confesses Christ "incarnate of the Holy Spirit and the Virgin Mary." But the birth of God from the Ever-Virgin was a stumbling stone for those who wished to call themselves Christians but did not wish to humble themselves in mind and be zealous for purity of life. The pure life of Mary was a reproach for those who were impure also in their thoughts. So as to show themselves Christians, they did not dare to deny that Christ was born of a Virgin, but they began to affirm that Mary remained a virgin only *until she brought forth her first-born son, Jesus* (Matt. 1:25).

"After the birth of Jesus," said the false teacher Helvidius in the 4th century, and likewise many others before and after him, "Mary entered into conjugal life with Joseph and had from him children, who are called in the Gospels the brothers and sisters of Christ." But the word "until" does not signify that Mary remained a virgin only until a certain time. The word "until" and words similar to it often signify eternity. In the Sacred Scripture it is said of Christ: *In His days shall shine forth righteousness and an abundance of peace,* until *the moon be taken away* (Ps. 71:7), but this does not mean that when there shall no longer be a moon at the end of the world, God's righteousness shall no longer be; precisely then, rather, will it triumph. And what does it mean when it says: *For He must reign,* until *He hath put all enemies under His feet?* (I Cor. 15:25). Is the Lord then to reign only for the time until His enemies shall be under His feet?! And David, in the fourth Psalm of the Ascents says: *As the eyes of the handmaid look unto the hands of her mistress, so do our eyes look unto the Lord our God,* until *He take pity on us* (Ps. 122:2). Thus, the Prophet will have his eyes toward the Lord until he obtains mercy, but having obtained it he will direct them to the earth? (Blessed Jerome, "On the Ever-Virginity of Blessed Mary.") The Saviour in the Gospel says to the Apostles (Matt. 28:20): *Lo, I am with you always, even* unto *the end of the world.* Thus, after the end of the world the Lord will step away from His disciples, and then, when they shall judge the twelve tribes of Israel upon twelve thrones, they will not have the promised communion with the Lord? (Blessed Jerome, op. cit.)

It is likewise incorrect to think that the brothers and sisters of Christ were the children of His Most Holy Mother. The names of "brother" and "sister" have several distinct meanings. Signifying a certain kinship between people or their spiritual closeness, these words are used sometimes in a broader, and sometimes in a narrower sense. In any case, people are called brothers or sisters if they have a common father and mother, or only a common father or mother; or even if they have different fathers and mothers, if their parents later (having become widowed) have entered into marriage (stepbrothers); or if their parents are bound by close degrees of kinship.

In the Gospel it can nowhere be seen that those who are called there the brothers of Jesus were or were considered the children of His Mother. On the contrary, it was known that James and others were the sons of Joseph, the Betrothed of Mary, who was a widower with children from his first wife. (St. Epiphanius of Cyprus, *Panarion,* 78.) Likewise, the sister of His Mother, Mary the wife of Cleopas, who stood with Her at the Cross of the Lord (John 19:25), also had children, who in view of such close kinship with full right could also be called brothers of the Lord. That the so-called brothers and sisters of the Lord were not the children of His Mother is clearly evident from the fact that the Lord entrusted His Mother before His death to His beloved disciple John. Why should He do this if She had other children besides Him? They themselves would have taken care of Her. The sons of Joseph, the supposed father of Jesus, did not consider themselves obliged to take care of one they regarded as their stepmother, or at least did not have for Her such love as blood children have for parents, and such as the adopted John had for Her.

Thus, a careful study of Sacred Scripture reveals with complete clarity the insubstantiality of the objections against the Ever-Virginity of Mary and puts to shame those who teach differently.

Icon of the Mother of God "Joy of All Who Sorrow."
18th-century copy now in New York City, showing the
Mother of God surrounded by various saints.

IV

The Nestorian Heresy and The Third Ecumenical Council

WHEN ALL THOSE who had dared to speak against the sanctity and purity of the Most Holy Virgin Mary had been reduced to silence, an attempt was made to destroy Her veneration as *Mother of God.* In the 5th century the Archbishop of Constantinople, Nestorius, began to preach that of Mary had been born only the man Jesus, in Whom the Divinity had taken abode and dwelt in Him as in a temple. At first he allowed his presbyter Anastasius and then he himself began to teach openly in church that one should not call Mary "Theotokos," since She had not given birth to the God-Man. He considered it demeaning for himself to worship a child wrapped in swaddling clothes and lying in a manger.

Such sermons evoked a universal disturbance and unease over the purity of faith, at first in Constantinople and then everywhere else where rumors of the new teaching spread. St. Proclus, the disciple of St. John Chrysostom, who was then Bishop of Cyzicus and later Archbishop of Constantinople, in the presence of Nestorius gave in church a sermon in which he confessed the Son of God born in the flesh of the Virgin, Who in truth is the Theotokos (Birthgiver of God), for already in the womb of the Most Pure One, at the time of Her conception, the Divinity was united with the Child conceived of the Holy Spirit; and this Child, even though He was born of the Virgin Mary only in His human nature, still was born already true God and true man.

Nestorius stubbornly refused to change his teaching, saying that one must distinguish between Jesus and the Son of God, that Mary should not be called Theotokos, but Christotokos (Birthgiver of Christ), since the Jesus Who was born of Mary was only the man Christ (which signifies Messiah, anointed one), like to God's anointed ones of old, the prophets, only surpassing them in fullness of communion with God. The teaching of Nestorius thus constituted a denial of the whole economy of God, for if from Mary only a man was born, then it was not God Who suffered for us, but a man.

St. Cyril, Archbishop of Alexandria, finding out about the teaching of Nestorius and about the church disorders evoked by this teaching in Constantinople, wrote a letter to Nestorius, in which he tried to persuade him to hold the teaching which the Church had confessed from its foundation, and not to introduce anything novel into this teaching. In addition, St. Cyril wrote to the clergy and people of Constantinople that they should be firm in the Orthodox faith and not fear the persecutions by Nestorius against those who were not in agreement with him. St. Cyril also wrote informing of everything to Rome, to the holy Pope Celestine, who with all his flock was then firm in Orthodoxy.

St. Celestine for his part wrote to Nestorius and called upon him to preach the Orthodox faith, and not his own. But Nestorius remained deaf to all persuasion and replied that what he was preaching *was* the Orthodox faith, while his opponents were heretics. St. Cyril wrote Nestorius again and composed twelve anathemas, that is, set forth in twelve paragraphs the chief

Icon of the Theotokos
"The Life-giving Spring."

differences of the Orthodox teaching from the teaching preached by Nestorius, acknowledging as excommunicated from the Church everyone who should reject even a single one of the paragraphs he had composed.

Nestorius rejected the whole of the text composed by St. Cyril and wrote his own exposition of the teaching which he preached, likewise in twelve paragraphs, giving over to anathema (that is, excommunication from the Church) everyone who did not accept it. The danger to purity of faith was increasing all the time. St. Cyril wrote a letter to Theodosius the Younger, who was then reigning, to his wife Eudocia and to the Emperor's sister Pulcheria, entreating them likewise to concern themselves with ecclesiastical matters and restrain the heresy.

It was decided to convene an *Ecumenical Council,* at which hierarchs, gathered from the ends of the world, should decide whether the faith preached by Nestorius was Orthodox. As the place for the council, which was to be the Third Ecumenical Council, they chose the city of Ephesus, in which the Most Holy Virgin Mary had once dwelt together with the Apostle John the Theologian. St. Cyril gathered his fellow bishops in Egypt and together with them travelled by sea to Ephesus. From Antioch overland came John, Archbishop of Antioch, with the Eastern bishops. The Bishop of Rome, St. Celestine, could not go himself and asked St. Cyril to defend the Orthodox faith, and in addition he sent from himself two bishops and the presbyter of the Roman Church Philip, to whom he also gave instructions as to what to say. To Ephesus there came likewise Nestorius and the bishops of the Constantinople region, and the bishops of Palestine, Asia Minor, and Cyprus.

On the 10th of the calends of July according to the Roman reckoning, that is, June 22, 431, in the Ephesian Church of the Virgin Mary, the bishops assembled, headed by the Bishop of Alexandria, Cyril, and the Bishop of Ephesus, Memnon, and took their places. In their midst was placed a Gospel as a sign of the invisible headship of the Ecumenical Council by Christ Himself. At first the Symbol of Faith which had been composed by the First and Second Ecumenical Councils was read; then there was read to the Council the Imperial Proclamation which was brought by the representatives of the Emperors Theodosius and Valentinian, Emperors of the Eastern and Western parts of the Empire.

The Imperial Proclamation having been heard, the reading of documents began, and there were read the Epistles of Cyril and Celestine to Nestorius, as well as the replies of Nestorius. The Council, by the lips of its members, acknowledged the teaching of Nestorius to be impious and condemned it, acknowledging Nestorius as deprived of his See and of the priesthood. A decree was composed concerning this which was signed by about 160 participants of the Council; and since some of them represented also other bishops who did not have the opportunity to be personally at the Council, the decree of the Council was actually the decision of more than 200 bishops, who had their Sees in the various regions of the Church at that time, and they testified that they confessed the Faith which from all antiquity had been kept in their localities.

Thus the decree of the Council was the voice of the Ecumenical Church, which clearly expressed its faith that Christ, born of the Virgin, is the true God Who became man; and inasmuch as Mary gave birth to the perfect Man Who was at the same time perfect God, She rightly should be revered as THEOTOKOS.

At the end of the session its decree was immediately communicated to the waiting people. The whole of Ephesus rejoiced when it found out that the veneration of the Holy Virgin had been defended, for She was especially revered in this city, of which She had been a resident during Her earthly life and a Patroness after Her departure into eternal life. The people greeted the Fathers ecstatically when in the evening they returned home after the session. They accompanied them to their homes with lighted torches and burned incense in the streets. Everywhere were to be heard joyful greetings, the glorification of the Ever-Virgin, and the praises of the Fathers who had defended Her name against the heretics. The decree of the Council was displayed in the streets of Ephesus.

The Council had five more sessions, on June 10 and 11, July 16, 17, and 22, and August 31. At these sessions there were set forth, in six canons, measures for action against those who would dare to spread the teaching of Nestorius and change the decree of the Council of Ephesus.

At the complaint of the bishops of Cyprus against the pretensions of the Bishop of Antioch, the Council decreed that the Church of Cyprus should preserve its independence in Church government, which it had possessed from the Apostles, and that in general none of the bishops should subject to themselves regions which had been previously independent from them, "lest under the pretext of priesthood the pride of earthly power should steal in, and lest we lose, ruining it little by little, the freedom which our Lord Jesus Christ, the Deliverer of all men, has given us by His Blood."

The Council likewise confirmed the condemnation of the Pelagian heresy, which taught that man can be saved by his own powers without the necessity of having the grace of God. It also decided certain matters of church government, and addressed epistles to the bishops who had not attended the Council, announcing its decrees and calling upon all to stand on guard for the Orthodox Faith and the peace of the Church. At the same time the Council acknowledged that the teaching of the Orthodox Ecumenical Church had been fully and clearly enough set forth in the Nicaeo-Constantinopolitan Symbol of Faith, which is why it itself did not compose a new Symbol of Faith and forbade in future "to compose another Faith," that is, to compose other Symbols of Faith or make changes in the Symbol which had been confirmed at the Second Ecumenical Council.

This latter decree was violated several centuries later by Western Christians when, at first in separate places, and then throughout the whole Roman Church, there was made to the Symbol the addition that the Holy Spirit proceeds "and from the Son," which addition has been approved by the Roman Popes from the 11th century, even though up until that time their predecessors, beginning with St. Celestine, firmly kept to the decision of the Council of Ephesus, which was the Third Ecumenical Council, and fulfilled it.

Thus the peace which had been destroyed by Nestorius settled once more in the Church. The true Faith had been defended and false teaching accused.

The Council of Ephesus is rightly venerated as Ecumenical, on the same level as the Councils of Nicaea and Constantinople which preceded it. At it there were present representatives of the whole Church. Its decisions were accepted by the whole Church "from one end of the universe to the other." At it there was confessed the teaching which had been held from Apostolic times. The Council did not create a new teaching, but it loudly testified of the truth which some had tried to replace by an invention. It precisely set forth the confession of the Divinity of Christ Who was born of the Virgin. The belief of the Church and its judgment on this question were now so clearly expressed that no one could any longer ascribe to the Church his own false reasonings. In the future there could arise other questions demanding the decision of the whole Church, but not the question *whether Jesus Christ were God.*

Subsequent Councils based themselves in their decisions on the decrees of the Councils which had preceded them. They did not compose a new Symbol of Faith, but only gave an explanation of it. At the Third Ecumenical Council there was firmly and clearly confessed *the teaching of the Church concerning the Mother of God.* Previously the Holy Fathers had accused those who had slandered the immaculate life of the Virgin Mary; and now concerning those who had tried to lessen Her honor it was proclaimed to all: "He who does not confess Immanuel to be true God and therefore the Holy Virgin to be Theotokos, because She gave birth in the flesh to the Word Who is from God the Father and Who became flesh, let him be anathema (separated from the Church)" (First Anathema of St. Cyril of Alexandria).

Icon of the "Protection of the Theotokos," Novgorod School,
showing St. Andrew the Fool for Christ and his disciple
on the lower right.

V

Attempts of Iconoclasts to Lessen The Glory of the Queen of Heaven; They Are Put to Shame

AFTER THE THIRD Ecumenical Council, Christians began yet more fervently, both in Constantinople and in other places, to hasten to the intercession of the Mother of God and their hopes in Her intercession were not vain. She manifested Her help to innumerable sick people, helpless people, and those in misfortune. Many times She appeared as defender of Constantinople against outward enemies, once even showing in visible fashion to St. Andrew the Fool for Christ Her wondrous Protection over the people who were praying at night in the Temple of Blachernae.

The Queen of Heaven gave victory in battles to the Byzantine Emperors, which is why they had the custom to take with them in their campaigns Her Icon of Hodigitria (Guide). She strengthened ascetics and zealots of Christian life in their battle against human passions and weaknesses. She enlightened and instructed the Fathers and Teachers of the Church, including St. Cyril of Alexandria himself when he was hesitating to acknowledge the innocence and sanctity of St. John Chrysostom.

The Most Pure Virgin placed hymns in the mouths of the composers of church hymns, sometimes making renowned singers out of the untalented who had no gift of song, but who were pious laborers, such as St. Romanus the Sweet-Singer (the Melodist). Is it therefore surprising that Christians strove to magnify the name of their constant Intercessor? In Her honor feasts were established, to Her were dedicated wondrous songs, and Her Images were revered.

The malice of the prince of this world armed the sons of apostasy once more to raise battle against Immanuel and His Mother in this same Constantinople, which revered now, as Ephesus had previously, the Mother of God as its Intercessor. Not daring at first to speak openly against the Champion General, they wished to lessen Her glorification by forbidding the veneration of the Icons of Christ and His saints, calling this idol-worship. The Mother of God now also strengthened zealots of piety in the battle for the veneration of Images, manifesting many signs from Her Icons and healing the severed hand of St. John of Damascus who had written in defence of the Icons.

The persecution against the venerators of Icons and Saints ended again in the victory and triumph of Orthodoxy, for the veneration given to the Icons ascends to those who are depicted in them; and the holy ones of God are venerated as friends of God for the sake of the Divine grace which dwelt in them, in accordance with the words of the Psalm: "Most precious to me are Thy friends." The Most Pure Mother of God was glorified with special honor in heaven and on earth, and She, even in the days of the mocking of the holy Icons, manifested through them so many wondrous miracles that even today we remember them with contrition. The hymn "In Thee All Creation Rejoices, O Thou Who Art Full of Grace," and the Icon of the Three Hands remind us of the healing of St. John Damascene before this Icon; the depiction of the Iveron Icon of the Mother of God reminds us of the miraculous deliverance from enemies by this Icon, which had been thrown in the sea by a widow who was unable to save it.

No persecutions against those who venerated the Mother of God and all that is bound up with the memory of Her could lessen the love of Christians for their Intercessor. The rule was established that every series of hymns in the Divine services should end with a hymn or verse in honor of the Mother of God (the so-called "Theotokia"). Many times in the year Christians in all corners of the world gather together in church, as before they gathered together, to praise Her, to thank Her for the benefactions She has shown, and to beg mercy.

But could the adversary of Christians, the devil, who *goeth about roaring like a lion, seeking whom he may devour* (I Peter 5:8), remain an indifferent spectator to the glory of the Immaculate One? Could he acknowledge himself as defeated, and cease to wage warfare against the truth through men who do his will? And so, when all the universe resounded with the good news of the Faith of Christ, when everywhere the name of the Most Holy One was invoked, when the earth was filled with churches, when the houses of Christians were adorned with Icons depicting Her—then there appeared and began to spread a new false teaching about the Mother of God. This false teaching is dangerous in that many cannot immediately understand to what degree it undermines the true veneration of the Mother of God.

"In Thee All Creation Rejoices." 16th-century Icon from
Solovki Monastery, Russia.

VI

Zeal Not According to Knowledge

(Romans 10:2)

*The corruption by the Latins, in the newly invented
dogma of the "Immaculate Conception," of the true
veneration of the Most Holy Mother of God
and Ever-Virgin Mary.*

WHEN THOSE WHO censured the immaculate life of
the Most Holy Virgin had been rebuked, as well as those who
denied Her Ever-virginity, those who denied Her dignity as the
Mother of God, and those who disdained Her Icons—then,
when the glory of the Mother of God had illuminated the whole
universe, there appeared a teaching which seemingly exalted
highly the Virgin Mary, but in reality *denied all Her virtues.*

This teaching is called that of the Immaculate Conception
of the Virgin Mary, and it was accepted by the followers of the
Papal throne of Rome. The teaching is this: that "the All-blessed
Virgin Mary in the first instant of Her Conception, by the
special grace of Almighty God and by a special privilege, for the
sake of the future merits of Jesus Christ, Saviour of the human
race, was preserved exempt from all stain of original sin" (Bull
of Pope Pius IX concerning the new dogma). In other words,
the Mother of God at Her very conception was preserved from

original sin and, by the grace of God, was placed in a state where it was impossible for Her to have personal sins.

Christians had not heard of this before the ninth century, when for the first time the Abbot of Corvey, Paschasius Radbertus, expressed the opinion that the Holy Virgin was conceived without original sin. Beginning from the 12th century, this idea begins to spread among the clergy and flock of the Western church, which had already fallen away from the Universal Church and thereby lost the grace of the Holy Spirit.

However, by no means all of the members of the Roman church agreed with the new teaching. There was a difference of opinion even among the most renowned theologians of the West, the pillars, so to speak, of the Latin church. Thomas Aquinas and Bernard of Clairvaux decisively censured it, while Duns Scotus defended it. From the teachers this division carried over to their disciples: the Latin Dominican monks, after their teacher Thomas Aquinas, preached against the teaching of the Immaculate Conception, while the followers of Duns Scotus, the Franciscans, strove to implant it everywhere. The battle between these two currents continued for the course of several centuries. Both on the one and on the other side there were those who were considered among the Catholics as the greatest authorities.

There was no help in deciding the question in the fact that several people declared that they had had a revelation from above concerning it. The nun Bridget [of Sweden], renowned in the 14th century among the Catholics, spoke in her writings about the appearances to her of the Mother of God, Who Herself told her that She had been conceived immaculately, without original sin. But her contemporary, the yet more renowned ascetic Catherine of Sienna, affirmed that in Her conception the Holy Virgin participated in original sin, concerning which she had received a revelation from Christ Himself. (See the book of Archpriest A. Lebedev, *Differences in the Teaching on the Most Holy Mother of God in the Churches of East and West.*)

Thus, neither on the foundation of theological writings, nor on the foundation of miraculous manifestations which contradicted each other, could the Latin flock distinguish for a long time where the truth was. Roman Popes until Sixtus IV (end of the 15th century) remained apart from these disputes, and only this Pope in 1475 approved a service in which the teaching of the Immaculate Conception was clearly expressed; and several years later he forbade a condemnation of those who believed in the Immaculate Conception. However, even Sixtus IV did not yet decide to affirm that such was the unwavering teaching of the church; and therefore, having forbidden the condemnation of those who believed in the Immaculate Conception, he also did not condemn those who believed otherwise.

Meanwhile, the teaching of the Immaculate Conception obtained more and more partisans among the members of the Roman church. The reason for this was the fact that it seemed more pious and pleasing to the Mother of God to give Her as much glory as possible. The striving of the people to glorify the Heavenly Intercessor, on the one hand, and on the other hand, the deviation of Western theologians into abstract speculations which led only to a seeming truth (Scholasticism), and finally, the patronage of the Roman Popes after Sixtus IV—all this led to the fact that the opinion concerning the Immaculate Conception which had been expressed by Paschasius Radbertus in the 9th century was already the general belief of the Latin church in the 19th century. There remained only to proclaim this definitely as the church's teaching, which was done by the Roman Pope Pius IX during a solemn service on December 8, 1854, when he declared that the Immaculate Conception of the Most Holy Virgin was a dogma of the Roman church.

Thus the Roman church added yet another deviation from the teaching which it had confessed while it was a member of the Catholic, Apostolic Church, which faith has been held up to now unaltered and unchanged by the Orthodox Church. The proclamation of the new dogma satisfied the broad masses of people who belonged to the Roman church, who in simplicity of heart thought that the proclamation of the new teaching in the church would serve for the greater glory of the Mother of God, to Whom by this they were making a gift, as it were. There was also satisfied the vainglory of the Western theologians who defended and worked it out. But most of all the proclamation of the new dogma was profitable for the Roman throne itself, since, having proclaimed the new dogma by his own authority, even though he did listen to the opinions of the bishops of the Catholic church, the Roman Pope by this very fact openly appropriated to himself the right to change the teaching of the Roman church and placed his own voice above the testimony of Sacred Scripture and Tradition. A direct deduction from this was the fact that the Roman Popes were infallible in matters of faith, which indeed this very same Pope Pius IX likewise proclaimed as a dogma of the Catholic church in 1870.

Thus was the teaching of the Western church changed after it had fallen away from communion with the True Church. It has introduced into itself newer and newer teachings, thinking by this to glorify the Truth yet more, but in reality distorting it. While the Orthodox Church humbly confesses what it has received from Christ and the Apostles, the Roman church dares to add to it, sometimes from *zeal not according to knowledge* (cf. Rom. 10:2), and sometimes by deviating into superstitions and into the *contradictions of knowledge falsely so called* (I Tim. 6:20). It could not be otherwise. That *the gates of hell shall not prevail* against the Church (Matt. 16:18) is promised only to the True, Universal Church; but upon those who have fallen away from it are fulfilled the words: *As the branch cannot bear fruit of itself, except it abide in the vine; so neither can ye, except ye abide in Me* (John 15:4).

It is true that in the very definition of the new dogma it is said that a new teaching is not being established, but that there is only being proclaimed as the church's that which always existed in the church and which has been held by many Holy Fathers, excerpts from whose writings are cited. However, all the cited references speak only of the exalted sanctity of the Virgin Mary and of Her immaculateness, and give Her various names which define Her purity and spiritual might; but nowhere is there any word of the immaculateness of Her conception. Meanwhile, these same Holy Fathers in other places say that only Jesus Christ is completely pure of every sin, while all men, being born of Adam, have borne a flesh subject to the law of sin.

None of the ancient Holy Fathers say that God in miraculous fashion purified the Virgin Mary while yet in the womb; and many directly indicate that the Virgin Mary, just as all men, endured a battle with sinfulness, but was victorious over temptations and was saved by Her Divine Son.

Commentators of the Latin confession likewise say that the Virgin Mary was saved by Christ. But they understand this in the sense that Mary was preserved from the taint of original sin in view of the future merits of Christ (Bull on the Dogma of the Immaculate Conception). The Virgin Mary, according to their teaching, received in advance, as it were, the gift which Christ brought to men by His sufferings and death on the Cross. Moreover, speaking of the torments of the Mother of God which She endured standing at the Cross of Her Beloved Son, and in general of the sorrows with which the life of the Mother of God was filled, they consider them an addition to the sufferings of Christ and consider Mary to be our *Co-Redemptress.*

According to the commentary of the Latin theologians, "Mary is an associate with our Redeemer as Co-Redemptress" (see Lebedev, op. cit. p. 273). "In the act of Redemption, She, in a certain way, helped Christ" (Catechism of Dr. Weimar). "The Mother of God," writes Dr. Lentz, "bore the burden of Her martyrdom not merely courageously, but also joyfully, even though with a broken heart" (Mariology of Dr. Lentz). For this reason, She is "a complement of the Holy Trinity," and "just as Her Son is the only Intermediary chosen by God between His offended majesty and sinful men, so also, precisely, the chief Mediatress placed by Him between His Son and us is the Blessed Virgin." "In three respects—as Daughter, as Mother, and as Spouse of God—the Holy Virgin is exalted to a certain equality with the Father, to a certain superiority over the Son, to a certain nearness to the Holy Spirit" ("The Immaculate Conception," Malou, Bishop of Brouges).

Thus, according to the teaching of the representatives of Latin theology, the Virgin Mary in the work of Redemption is placed side by side with Christ Himself and is exalted to an *equality with God.* One cannot go farther than this. If all this has not been definitively formulated as a dogma of the Roman church as yet, still the Roman Pope Pius IX, having made the first step in this direction, has shown the direction for the further development of the generally recognized teaching of his church, and has indirectly confirmed the above-cited teaching about the Virgin Mary.

Thus the Roman church, in its strivings to exalt the Most Holy Virgin, is going on the path of complete *deification* of Her. And if even now its authorities call Mary a complement of the Holy Trinity, one may soon expect that the Virgin will be revered like God.

There have entered on this same path a group of thinkers who for the time being, belong to the Orthodox Church, but who are building a new theological system having as its foundation the philosophical teaching of Sophia, Wisdom, as a special power binding the Divinity and the creation. Likewise developing the teaching of the dignity of the Mother of God, they wish to see in Her an Essence which is some kind of mid-point between God and man. In some questions they are more moderate than the Latin theologians, but in others, if you please, they have already left them behind. While denying the teaching of the Immaculate Conception and the freedom from original sin, they still teach Her full freedom from any personal sins, seeing in Her an Intermediary between men and God, like Christ: in the person of Christ there has appeared on earth the Second Person of the Holy Trinity, the Pre-eternal Word, the Son of God; while the Holy Spirit is manifest through the Virgin Mary.

In the words of one of the representatives of this tendency, when the Holy Spirit came to dwell in the Virgin Mary, she acquired "a dyadic life, human and divine; that is, She was completely deified, because in Her hypostatic being was manifest the living, creative revelation of the Holy Spirit" (Archpriest Sergei Bulgakov, *The Unburnt Bush,* 1927, p.154). "She is a perfect manifestation of the Third Hypostasis" (Ibid., p. 175), "a creature, but also no longer a creature" (p.191). This striving towards the deification of the Mother of God is to be observed primarily in the West, where at the same time, on the other hand, various sects of a Protestant character are having great success, together with the chief branches of Protestantism, Lutheranism and Calvinism, which in general deny the veneration of the Mother of God and the calling upon Her in prayer.

But we can say with the words of St. Epiphanius of Cyprus: "There is an equal harm in both these heresies, both when men demean the Virgin and when, on the contrary, they glorify Her beyond what is proper" (*Panarion,* "Against the Collyridians").

This Holy Father accuses those who give Her an almost divine worship: "Let Mary be in honor, but let *worship* be given to the Lord" (same source). "Although Mary is a chosen vessel, still She was a woman by nature, not to be distinguished at all from others. Although the history of Mary and Tradition relate that it was said to Her father Joachim in the desert, 'Thy wife hath conceived,' still this was done not without marital union and not without the seed of man" (same source). "One should not revere the saints above what is proper, but should revere their Master. Mary is not God, and did not receive a body from heaven, but from the joining of man and woman; and according to the promise, like Isaac, She was prepared to take part in the Divine Economy. But, on the other hand, let none dare foolishly to offend the Holy Virgin" (St. Epiphanius, "Against the Antidikomarionites").

The Orthodox Church, highly exalting the Mother of God in its hymns of praise, does not dare to ascribe to Her that which has not been communicated about Her by Sacred Scripture or Tradition. "Truth is foreign to all overstatements as well as to all understatements. It gives to everything a fitting measure and fitting place" (Bishop Ignatius Brianchaninov). Glorifying the immaculateness of the Virgin Mary and the manful bearing of sorrows in Her earthly life, the Fathers of the Church, on the other hand, reject the idea that She was an intermediary between God and men in the sense of the joint Redemption by Them of the human race. Speaking of Her preparedness to die together with Her Son and to suffer together with Him for the sake of the salvation of all, the renowned Father of the Western Church, Saint Ambrose, Bishop of Milan, adds: "But the sufferings of Christ did not need any help, as the Lord Himself prophesied concerning this long before: *I looked about, and there was none to help; I sought and there was none to give aid: therefore My arm delivered them* (Is. 63:5)." (St. Ambrose, "Concerning the Upbringing of the Virgin and the Ever-Virginity of Holy Mary," ch. 7).

This same Holy Father teaches concerning the universality of original sin, from which Christ alone is an exception. "Of all those born of women, there is not a single one who is perfectly holy, apart from the Lord Jesus Christ, Who in a special new way of immaculate birthgiving, did not experience earthly taint" (St. Ambrose, *Commentary on Luke,* ch. 2). "God alone is without sin. All born in the usual manner of woman and man, that is, of fleshly union, become guilty of sin. Consequently, He Who does not have sin was not conceived in this manner" (St. Ambrose, Ap. Aug. "Concerning Marriage and Concupiscence"). "One Man alone, the Intermediary between God and man, is free from the bonds of sinful birth, because He was born of a Virgin, and because in being born He did not experience the touch of sin" (St. Ambrose, ibid., Book 2: "Against Julianus").

Another renowned teacher of the Church, especially revered in the West, Blessed Augustine, writes: "As for other men, excluding Him Who is the cornerstone, I do not see for them any other means to become temples of God and to be dwellings for God apart from spiritual rebirth, which must absolutely be preceded by fleshly birth. Thus, no matter how much we might think about children who are in the womb of the mother, and even though the word of the holy Evangelist who says of John the Baptist that he leaped for joy in the womb of his mother (which occurred not otherwise than by the action of the Holy Spirit), or the word of the Lord Himself spoken to Jeremiah: *I have sanctified thee before thou didst leave the womb of thy mother* (Jer. 1:5)— no matter how much these might or might not give us basis for thinking that children in this condition are capable of a certain sanctification, still in any case it cannot be doubted that the sanctification by which all of us together and each of us separately become the temple of God is possible only for those who are reborn, and rebirth always presupposes birth. Only those who have already been born can be united with Christ and be in union with this Divine Body which makes His Church the living temple of the majesty of God" (Blessed Augustine, Letter 187).

The above-cited words of the ancient teachers of the Church testify that in the West itself the teaching which is now spread there was earlier rejected there. Even after the falling away of the Western church, Bernard, who is acknowledged there as a great authority, wrote, " I am frightened now, seeing that certain of you have desired to change the condition of important matters, introducing a new festival unknown to the Church, unapproved by reason, unjustified by ancient tradition. Are we really more learned and more pious than our fathers? You will say, 'One must glorify the Mother of God as much as possible.' This is true; but the glorification given to the Queen of Heaven demands discernment. This Royal Virgin does not have need of false glorifications, possessing as She does true crowns of glory and signs of dignity. Glorify the purity of Her flesh and the sanctity of Her life. Marvel at the abundance of the gifts of this Virgin; venerate Her Divine Son; exalt Her Who conceived without knowing concupiscence and gave birth without knowing pain. But what does one yet need to add to these dignities? People say that one must revere the conception which preceded the glorious birth-giving; for if the conception had not preceded, the birth-giving also would not have been glorious. But what would one say if anyone for the same reason should demand the same kind of veneration of the father and mother of Holy Mary? One might equally demand the same for Her grandparents and great-grandparents, to infinity. Moreover, how can there not be sin in the place where there was concupiscence? All the more, let one not say that the Holy Virgin was conceived of the Holy Spirit and not of man. I say decisively that the Holy Spirit descended upon Her, but not that He came with Her."

"I say that the Virgin Mary could not be sanctified before Her conception, inasmuch as She did not exist. If, all the more, She could not be sanctified in the moment of Her conception by reason of the sin which is inseparable from conception, then it remains to believe that She was sanctified after She was conceived in the womb of Her mother. This sanctification, if it annihilates sin, makes holy Her birth, but not Her conception. No one is given the right to be conceived in sanctity; only the Lord Christ was conceived of the Holy Spirit, and He alone is holy from His very conception. Excluding Him, it is to all the descendants of Adam that must be referred that which one of them says of himself, both out of a feeling of humility and in acknowledgement of the truth: *Behold I was conceived in iniquities* (Ps. 50:7). How can one demand that this conception be holy, when it was not the work of the Holy Spirit, not to mention that it came from concupiscence? The Holy Virgin, of course, rejects that glory which, evidently, glorifies sin. She cannot in any way justify a novelty invented in spite of the teaching of the Church, a novelty which is the mother of imprudence, the sister of unbelief, and the daughter of light-mindedness" (Bernard, Epistle 174; cited, as were the references from Blessed Augustine, from Lebedev). The above-cited words clearly reveal both the novelty and the absurdity of the new dogma of the Roman church.

The teaching of the complete sinlessness of the Mother of God (1) does not correspond to Sacred Scripture, where there is repeatedly mentioned the sinlessness of the *One Mediator between God and man, the man Jesus Christ* (I Tim. 2:5); *and in Him is no sin* (I John 3:5); *Who did no sin, neither was guile found in His mouth* (I Peter 2:22); *One that hath been in all points tempted like as we are, yet without sin* (Heb. 4:15); *Him Who knew no sin, He made to be sin on our behalf* (II Cor. 5:21). But concerning the rest of men it is said, *Who is pure of defilement? No one who has lived a single day of his life on earth* (Job 14:4). *God commendeth His own love toward us in that, while we were yet sinners, Christ died for us..... If, while we were enemies, we were reconciled to God through the death of His Son, much more, being reconciled, shall we be saved by His life* (Rom. 5:8-10).

(2) This teaching contradicts also *Sacred Tradition,* which is contained in numerous Patristic writings, where there is mentioned the exalted sanctity of the Virgin Mary from Her very birth, as well as Her cleansing by the Holy Spirit at Her conception of Christ, but not at Her own conception by Anna. "There is none without stain before Thee, even though his life be but a day, save Thee alone, Jesus Christ our God, Who didst appear on earth without sin, and through Whom we all trust to obtain mercy and the remission of sins" (St. Basil the Great, Third Prayer of Vespers of Pentecost). "But when Christ came through a pure, virginal, unwedded, God-fearing, undefiled Mother without wedlock and without father, and inasmuch as it befitted Him to be born, He purified the female nature, rejected the bitter Eve and overthrew the laws of the flesh" (St. Gregory the Theologian, "In Praise of Virginity"). However, even then, as Sts. Basil the Great and John Chrysostom speak of this, She was not placed in the state of being unable to sin, but continued to take care for Her salvation and overcame all temptations (St. John Chrysostom, *Commentary on John,* Homily 85; St. Basil the Great, Epistle 160).

(3) The teaching that the Mother of God was purified before Her birth, so that from Her might be born the Pure Christ, is meaningless; because if the Pure Christ could be born only if the Virgin might be born pure, it would be necessary that Her parents also should be pure of original sin, and they again would

have to be born of purified parents, and going further in this way, one would have to come to the conclusion that Christ could not have become incarnate unless all His ancestors in the flesh, right up to Adam inclusive, had been purified beforehand of original sin. But then there would not have been any need for the very Incarnation of Christ, since Christ came down to earth in order to annihilate sin.

(4) The teaching that the Mother of God was preserved from original sin, as likewise the teaching that She was preserved by God's grace from personal sins, *makes God unmerciful and unjust;* because if God could preserve Mary from sin and purify Her before Her birth, then why does He not purify other men before their birth, but rather leaves them in sin? It follows likewise that God saves men apart from their will, predetermining certain ones before their birth to salvation.

(5) This teaching, which seemingly has the aim of exalting the Mother of God, in reality completely *denies all Her virtues.* After all, if Mary, even in the womb of Her mother, when She could not even desire anything either good or evil, was preserved by God's grace from every impurity, and then by that grace was preserved from sin even after Her birth, then in what does Her merit consist? If She could have been placed in the state of being unable to sin, and did not sin, then for what did God glorify Her? If She, without any effort, and without having any kind of impulses to sin, remained pure, then why is She crowned more than everyone else? There is no victory without an adversary.

The righteousness and sanctity of the Virgin Mary were manifested in the fact that She, being "human with passions like us," so loved God and gave Herself over to Him, that by Her purity She was exalted high above the rest of the human race. For this, having been foreknown and forechosen, She was vouchsafed to be purified by the Holy Spirit Who came upon

Her, and to conceive of Him the very Saviour of the world. The teaching of the grace-given sinlessness of the Virgin Mary denies Her victory over temptations; from a victor who is worthy to be crowned with crowns of glory, this makes Her a blind instrument of God's Providence.

It is not an exaltation and greater glory, but a *belittlement* of Her, this "gift" which was given Her by Pope Pius IX and all the rest who think they can glorify the Mother of God by seeking out new truths. The Most Holy Mary has been so much glorified by God Himself, so exalted is Her life on earth and Her glory in heaven, that human inventions cannot add anything to Her honor and glory. That which people themselves invent only obscures Her Face from their eyes. *Brethren, take heed lest there shall be any one that maketh spoil of you through philosophy and vain deceit, after the tradition of men, after the rudiments of the world, and not after Christ,* wrote the Apostle Paul by the Holy Spirit (Col. 2:8).

Such a "vain deceit" is the teaching of the Immaculate Conception by Anna of the Virgin Mary, which at first sight exalts, but in actual fact belittles Her. Like every lie, it is a seed of the "father of lies" (John 8:44), the devil, who has succeeded by it in deceiving many who do not understand that they blaspheme the Virgin Mary. Together with it there should also be rejected all the other teachings which have come from it or are akin to it. The striving to exalt the Most Holy Virgin to an equality with Christ ascribing to Her maternal tortures at the Cross an equal significance with the sufferings of Christ, so that the Redeemer and "Co-Redemptress" suffered equally, according to the teaching of the Papists, or that "the human nature of the Mother of God in heaven together with the God-Man Jesus jointly reveal the full image of man" (Archpriest S. Bulgakov, *The Unburnt Bush,* p. 141)—is likewise a vain deceit and a seduction of philosophy. In Christ Jesus *there is neither male nor female* (Gal. 3:28), and Christ has redeemed the whole human race; therefore at His Resurrection equally did "Adam dance for joy and Eve rejoice" (Sunday Kontakia of the First and Third Tones), and by His Ascension did the Lord raise up the whole of human nature.

Likewise, that the Mother of God is a "complement of the Holy Trinity" or a "fourth Hypostasis"; that "the Son and the Mother are a revelation of the Father through the Second and Third Hypostases"; that the Virgin Mary is "a creature, but also no longer a creature"—all this is the fruit of vain, false wisdom which is not satisfied with what the Church has held from the time of the Apostles, but strives to glorify the Holy Virgin more than God has glorified Her.

Thus are the words of St. Epiphanius of Cyprus fulfilled: "Certain senseless ones in their opinion about the Holy Ever-Virgin have striven and are striving to put Her in place of God" (St. Epiphanius, "Against the Antidikomarionites"). But that which is offered to the Virgin in senselessness, instead of praise of Her, turns out to be blasphemy; and the All-Immaculate One rejects the lie, being the Mother of Truth (John 14:6).

Saints Joachim and Anna, the parents of the Theotokos.

VII

The Orthodox Veneration of The Mother of God

THE ORTHODOX CHURCH teaches about the Mother of God that which Sacred Tradition and Sacred Scripture have informed concerning Her, and daily it glorifies Her in its temples, asking Her help and defense. Knowing that She is pleased only by those praises which correspond to Her actual glory, the Holy Fathers and hymn-writers have entreated Her and Her Son to teach them how to hymn Her. "Set a rampart about my mind, O my Christ, for I make bold to sing the praise of Thy pure Mother" (Ikos of the Dormition). "The Church teaches that Christ was truly born of Mary the Ever-Virgin" (St. Epiphanius, "True Word Concerning the Faith"). "It is essential for us to confess that the Holy Ever-Virgin Mary is actually Theotokos (Birth-giver of God), so as not to fall into blasphemy. For those who deny that the Holy Virgin is actually Theotokos are no longer believers, but disciples of the Pharisees and Sadducees" (St. Ephraim the Syrian, "To John the Monk").

From Tradition it is known that Mary was the daughter of the aged Joachim and Anna, and that Joachim descended from the royal line of David, and Anna from the priestly line. Notwithstanding such a noble origin, they were poor. However, it was not this that saddened these righteous ones, but rather the fact that they did not have children and could not hope that their descendants would see the Messiah. And behold, when once, being disdained by the Hebrews for their barrenness, they both in grief of soul were offering up prayers to God—Joachim on a mountain to which he had retired after the priest did not want to offer his sacrifice in the Temple, and Anna in her own garden weeping over her barrenness—there appeared to them an angel who informed them that they would bring forth a daughter. Overjoyed, they promised to consecrate their child to God.

In nine months a daughter was born to them, called Mary, Who from Her early childhood manifested the best qualities of soul. When She was three years old, her parents, fulfilling their promise, solemnly led the little Mary to the Temple of Jerusalem; She Herself ascended the high steps and, by revelation from God, She was led into the very Holy of Holies, by the High Priest who met Her, taking with Her the grace of God which rested upon Her into the Temple which until then had been without grace. (See the Kontakion of the Entry into the Temple. This was the newly-built Temple into which the glory of God had not descended as it had upon the Ark or upon the Temple of Solomon.) She was settled in the quarters for virgins which existed in the Temple, but She spent so much time in prayer in the Holy of Holies that one might say that She lived in it. (Service to the Entry, second sticheron on "Lord, I have cried," and the "Glory, Both Now...") Being adorned with all virtues, She manifested an example of extraordinarily pure life. Being submissive and obedient to all, She offended no one, said no crude word to anyone, was friendly to all, and did not allow any unclean thought. (Abridged from St. Ambrose of Milan, "Concerning the Ever-Virginity of the Virgin Mary.")

"Despite the righteousness and the immaculateness of the life which the Mother of God led, *sin* and *eternal death* manifested their presence in Her. They could not but be manifested:

Such is the precise and faithful teaching of the Orthodox Church concerning the Mother of God with relation to original sin and death." (Bishop Ignatius Brianchaninov, "Exposition of the Teaching of the Orthodox Church on the Mother of God.") "A stranger to any fall into sin" (St. Ambrose of Milan, Commentary on the 118th Psalm), "She was not a stranger to sinful temptations." "God alone is without sin" (St. Ambrose, same source), "while man will always have in himself something yet needing correction and perfection in order to fulfill the commandment of God; *Be ye holy as I the Lord your God am Holy* (Leviticus 19:2). The more pure and perfect one is, the more he notices his imperfections and considers himself all the more unworthy.

The Virgin Mary, having given Herself entirely up to God, even though She repulsed from Herself every impulse to sin, still felt the weakness of human nature more powerfully than others and ardently desired the coming of the Saviour. In Her humility She considered Herself unworthy to be even the servant-girl of the Virgin Who was to give Him birth. So that nothing might distract Her from prayer and heedfulness to Herself, Mary gave to God a vow not to become married, in order to please only Him Her whole life long. Being betrothed to the elderly Joseph when Her age no longer allowed Her to remain in the Temple, She settled in his house in Nazareth. Here the Virgin was vouchsafed the coming of the Archangel Gabriel, who brought Her the good tidings of the birth from Her of the Son of the Most High. *Hail, Thou that art full of grace, the Lord is with Thee. Blessed art thou among women... The Holy Spirit shall come upon thee, and the power of the Most High shall overshadow thee: wherefore also that which is to be born shall be holy, and shall be called the Son of God* (Luke 1:28-35).

Mary received the angelic good tidings humbly and submissively. "Then the Word, in a way known to Himself, descended and, as He Himself willed, came and entered into Mary and abode in Her" (St. Ephraim the Syrian, "Praise of the Mother of God"). "As lightning illuminates what is hidden, so also Christ purifies what is hidden in the nature of things. He purified the Virgin also and then was born, so as to show that where Christ is, there is manifest purity in all its power. He purified the Virgin, having prepared Her by the Holy Spirit, and then the womb, having become pure, conceived Him. He purified the Virgin while She was inviolate; wherefore, having been born, He left Her virgin. I do not say that Mary became immortal, but that being illuminated by grace, She was not disturbed by sinful desires" (St. Ephraim the Syrian, Homily Against Heretics, 41). "The Light abode in Her, cleansed Her mind, made Her thoughts pure, made chaste Her concerns, sanctified Her virginity" (St. Ephraim the Syrian, "Mary and Eve"). "One who was pure according to human understanding, He made pure by grace" (Bishop Ignatius Brianchaninov, "Exposition of the Teaching of the Orthodox Church on the Mother of God").

Mary told no one of the appearance of the angel, but the angel himself revealed to Joseph concerning Mary's miraculous conception from the Holy Spirit (Matt. 1:18-25); and after the Nativity of Christ, with a multitude of the heavenly host, he announced it to the shepherds. The shepherds, coming to worship the new-born one, said that they had heard of Him. Having previously endured suspicion in silence, Mary now also listened in silence and *kept in Her heart* the sayings concerning the greatness of Her Son (Luke 2:8-19). She heard forty days later Symeon's prayer of praise and the prophecy concerning the weapon which would pierce Her soul. Later She saw how Jesus advanced in wisdom; She heard Him at the age of twelve teaching in the Temple, and everything She *kept in Her heart* (Luke 2:21-51).

Even though full of grace, She did not yet fully understand in what the service and the greatness of Her Son would consist. The Hebrew conceptions of the Messiah were still close to Her, and natural feelings forced Her to be concerned for Him, preserving Him from labors and dangers which it might seem, were excessive. Therefore She favored Her Son involuntarily at first, which evoked His indication of the superiority of spiritual to bodily kinship (Matt. 12:46-49). "He had concern also over the honor of His Mother, but much more over the salvation of Her soul and the good of men, for which He had become clothed in the flesh" (St. John Chrysostom, Commentary on John, Homily 21). Mary understood this and *heard the word of God and kept it* (Luke 11:27, 28). As no other person, She had the same feelings as Christ (Phil. 2:5), unmurmuringly bearing the grief of a mother when She saw Her Son persecuted and suffering. Rejoicing in the day of the Resurrection, on the day of Pentecost She was clothed with *power from on high* (Luke 24:49). The Holy Spirit Who descended upon Her *taught (Her) all things* (John 14:26), and *instructed (Her) in all truth* (John 16:13). Being enlightened, She began to labor all the more zealously to perform what She had heard from Her Son and Redeemer, so as to ascend to Him and to be with Him.

The end of the earthly life of the Most Holy Mother of God was the beginning of Her greatness. "Being adorned with Divine glory" (Irmos of the Canon of the Dormition), She stands and will stand, both in the day of the Last Judgment and in the future age, at the right hand of the throne of Her Son. She reigns with Him and has boldness towards Him as His Mother according to the flesh, and as one in spirit with Him, as one who performed the will of God and instructed others (Matt. 5:19). Merciful and full of love, She manifests Her love towards Her Son and God in love for the human race. She intercedes for it before the Merciful One, and going about the earth, She helps men.

Having experienced all the difficulties of earthly life, the Intercessor of the Christian race sees every tear, hears every groan and entreaty directed to Her. Especially near to Her are those who labor in the battle with the passions and are zealous for a God-pleasing life. But even in worldly cares She is an irreplaceable helper. "Joy of all who sorrow and intercessor for the offended, feeder of the hungry, consolation of travellers, harbor of the storm-tossed, visitation of the sick, protection and intercessor for the infirm, staff of old age, Thou art the Mother of God on high, O Most Pure One" (Sticheron of the Service to the Hodigitria). "The hope and intercession and refuge of Christians," "The Mother of God unceasing in prayers" (Kontakion of Dormition), "saving the world by Thine unceasing prayer" (Theotokion of the Third Tone). "She day and night doth pray for us, and the scepters of kingdoms are confirmed by Her prayers" (daily Nocturne).

There is no intellect or words to express the greatness of Her Who was born in the sinful human race but became "more honorable than the Cherubim and beyond compare more glorious than the Seraphim." "Seeing the grace of the secret mysteries of God made manifest and clearly fulfilled in the Virgin, I rejoice; and I know not how to understand the strange and secret manner whereby the Undefiled has been revealed as alone chosen above all creation, visible and spiritual. Therefore, wishing to praise Her, I am struck dumb with amazement in both mind and speech. Yet still I dare to proclaim and magnify Her: She is indeed the heavenly Tabernacle" (Ikos of the Entry into the Temple). "Every tongue is at a loss to praise Thee as is due; even a spirit from the world above is filled with dizziness, when it seeks to sing Thy praises, O Theotokos. But since Thou art good, accept our faith. Thou knowest well our love inspired by God, for Thou art the Protector of Christians, and we magnify Thee" (Irmos of the 9th Canticle, Service of the Theophany).

Icon of the Theotokos "Joy of All Joys," belonging to St. Seraphim of Sarov, before which he reposed in prayer in 1833. It is preserved today in Diveyevo Convent, Russia.

"Tenderness" ("Merciful and Man-loving") Icon of the Theotokos,
painted by the great 20th-century iconographer Pimen M. Sofronov.

AKATHIST

to our Most Holy Lady
the Mother of God

[The Akathist to the Theotokos is the highest expression of her veneration. Penned by St. Romanus the Melodist in the 6th century, it is used up to this day in its original form. The following translation was done by the late Archimandrite Lazarus Moore, who was in close association with Archbishop John Maximovitch; and it is likely that it was Archbishop John who commissioned the translation. Archimandrite Lazarus was a tireless laborer in transmitting authentic Orthodox spirituality, working for many years in India, Australia and California, and finally in Alaska, where he died and is buried. The movement of Orthodoxy in the English language is indebted to his zeal.]

KONTAKION 1

Queen of the Heavenly Host, Defender of our souls, we thy servants offer to thee songs of victory and thanksgiving, for thou, O Mother of God, hast delivered us from dangers. But as thou hast invincible power, free us from conflicts of all kinds that we may cry to thee:

Rejoice, unwedded Bride!

EIKOS 1

An Archangel was sent from Heaven to say to the Mother of God: Rejoice! And seeing Thee, O Lord, taking bodily form,

Vladimir Icon the Theotokos from Belozersk ("White Lake"), Russia. From the cell of St. Cyril of White Lake, before which this great Elder of the North poured out his heart in singing the Akathist to the Mother of God. During this singing, the Mother of God appeared to him and told him to found a monastery on White Lake.

he was amazed and with his bodiless voice he stood crying to her such things as these:

Rejoice, thou through whom joy will flash forth!

Rejoice, thou through whom the curse will cease!

Rejoice, revival of fallen Adam!

Rejoice, redemption of the tears of Eve!

Rejoice, height hard to climb for human thoughts!

Rejoice, depth hard to contemplate even for the eyes of Angels!

Rejoice, thou who art the King's throne!

Rejoice, thou who bearest Him Who bears all!

Rejoice, star that causest the Sun to appear!

Rejoice, womb of the divine incarnation!

Rejoice, thou through whom creation becomes new!

Rejoice, thou through whom the Creator becomes a babe!

Rejoice, unwedded Bride!

KONTAKION 2

Aware that she was living in chastity, the holy Virgin said boldly to Gabriel: "Thy strange message is hard for my soul to accept. How is it thou speakest of the birth from a seedless conception?" And she cried: Alleluia!

EIKOS 2

Seeking to know what passes knowledge, the Virgin cried to the ministering spirit: "Tell me, how can a son be born from a chaste womb?" Then he spoke to her in fear, only crying aloud thus:

Rejoice, initiate of God's ineffable will!

Rejoice, assurance of those who pray in silence!

Rejoice, prelude of Christ's miracles!

Rejoice, crown of His dogmas!

Rejoice, heavenly ladder by which God came down!

Rejoice, bridge that conveys us from earth to Heaven!
Rejoice, wonder of angels blazed abroad!
Rejoice, wound of demons bewailed afar!
Rejoice, thou who ineffably gavest birth to the Light!
Rejoice, thou who didst reveal thy secret to none!
Rejoice, thou who surpassest the knowledge of the wise!
Rejoice, thou who givest light to the minds of the faithful!
Rejoice, unwedded Bride!

KONTAKION 3

The power of the Most High then overshadowed the Virgin for conception, and showed her fruitful womb as a sweet meadow to all who wish to reap salvation, as they sing: Alleluia!

EIKOS 3

Pregnant with the Divine indwelling the Virgin ran to Elizabeth whose unborn babe at once recognized her embrace, rejoiced, and with leaps of joy as songs, cried to the Mother of God:
Rejoice, scion of an undying Shoot!
Rejoice, field of untainted fruit!
Rejoice, thou who laborest for Him Whose labor is love!
Rejoice, thou who givest birth to the Father of our life!
Rejoice, cornland yielding a rich crop of mercies!
Rejoice, table bearing a wealth of forgiveness!
Rejoice, thou who revivest the garden of delight!
Rejoice, thou who preparest a haven for souls!
Rejoice, acceptable incense of intercession!
Rejoice, purification of all the world!
Rejoice, favour of God to mortals!
Rejoice, access of mortals to God!
Rejoice, unwedded Bride!

KONTAKION 4

Sustaining from within a storm of doubtful thoughts, the chaste Joseph was troubled. For knowing thee to have no husband, he suspected a secret union, O Immaculate One. But when he learned that thy conception was of the Holy Spirit, he exclaimed: Alleluia!

EIKOS 4

The shepherds heard Angels carolling Christ's incarnate Presence, and running like sheep to their shepherd, they beheld him as an innocent Lamb fed at Mary's breast, and they sang to her and said:

Rejoice, mother of the Lamb and the Shepherd!

Rejoice, fold of spiritual sheep!

Rejoice, defence against invisible enemies!

Rejoice, key to the gates of Paradise!

Rejoice, for the things of Heaven rejoice with the earth!

Rejoice, for the things of earth join chorus with the Heavens!

Rejoice, never-silent voice of the Apostles!

Rejoice, invincible courage of the martyrs!

Rejoice, firm support of faith!

Rejoice, radiant blaze of grace!

Rejoice, thou through whom hell was stripped bare!

Rejoice, thou through whom we are clothed with glory!

Rejoice, unwedded Bride!

KONTAKION 5

Having sighted the divinely moving star, the Wise Men followed its light and held it as a lamp by which they sought a powerful King. And as they approached the Unapproachable, they rejoiced and shouted to Him: Alleluia!

EIKOS 5

The sons of the Chaldees saw in the hands of the Virgin Him Who with His hand made man. And knowing Him to be the Lord although He had taken the form of a servant, they hastened to worship Him with their gifts and cried to her who is blessed:

Rejoice, mother of the never-setting Star!
Rejoice, dawn of the mystic Day!
Rejoice, thou who didst extinguish the furnace of error!
Rejoice, thou who didst enlighten the initiates of the Trinity!
Rejoice, thou who didst banish from power the inhuman tyrant!
Rejoice, thou who hast shown us Christ as the Lord and Lover of men!
Rejoice, thou who redeemest from pagan worship!
Rejoice, thou who dost drag from the mire of works!
Rejoice, thou who hast stopped the worship of fire!
Rejoice, thou who hast quenched the flame of the passions!
Rejoice, guide of the faithful to chastity!
Rejoice, joy of all generations!
Rejoice, unwedded Bride!

KONTAKION 6

Turned God-bearing heralds, the Wise Men returned to Babylon. They fulfilled Thy prophecy and to all preached Thee as the Christ, and they left Herod as a trifler, who could not sing: Alleluia!

EIKOS 6

By shining in Egypt the light of truth, Thou didst dispel the darkness of falsehood, O Saviour. For, unable to endure Thy strength, its idols fell; and those who were freed from their spell cried to the Mother of God:

Rejoice, uplifting of men!
Rejoice, downfall of demons!
Rejoice, thou who hast trampled on the delusion of error!
Rejoice, thou who hast exposed the fraud of idols!
Rejoice, sea that has drowned the spiritual Pharaoh!
Rejoice, rock that has refreshed those thirsting for Life!
Rejoice, pillar of fire guiding those in darkness!
Rejoice, shelter of the world broader than a cloud!
Rejoice, sustenance replacing Manna!
Rejoice, minister of holy delight!
Rejoice, land of promise!
Rejoice, thou from whom flows milk and honey!
Rejoice, unwedded Bride!

KONTAKION 7

When Simeon was about to depart this life of delusion, Thou wast brought as a Babe to him. But he recognized Thee as also perfect God, and marvelling at Thy ineffable wisdom, he cried: Alleluia!

EIKOS 7

The Creator showed us a new creation when He appeared to us who came from Him. For He sprang from an unsown womb and kept it chaste as it was, that seeing the miracle we might sing to her and say:

Rejoice, flower of incorruption!
Rejoice, crown of continence!
Rejoice, flashing symbol of the resurrection!
Rejoice, mirror of the life of the Angels!
Rejoice, tree of glorious fruit by which the faithful are
    nourished!

Rejoice, bush of shady leaves by which many are sheltered!
Rejoice, thou who bearest the Guide of those astray!
Rejoice, thou who givest birth to the Redeemer of captives!
Rejoice, pleader before the Just Judge!
Rejoice, forgiveness of many sinners!
Rejoice, robe of freedom for the naked!
Rejoice, love that vanquishes all desire!
Rejoice, unwedded Bride!

KONTAKION 8

Seeing the Child Exile, let us be exiles from the world and transport our minds to Heaven. For the Most High God appeared on earth as lowly man, because He wished to draw to the heights those who cry to Him: Alleluia!

EIKOS 8

Wholly present was the infinite Word among those here below, yet in no way absent from those on high; for this was a divine condescension and not a change of place. And His birth was from a God-possessed Virgin who heard words like these:
Rejoice, container of the uncontainable God!
Rejoice, door of solemn mystery!
Rejoice, doubtful report of unbelievers!
Rejoice, undoubted boast of the faithful!
Rejoice, all-holy chariot of Him Who rides on the Cherubim!
Rejoice, all-glorious temple of Him Who is above the Seraphim!
Rejoice, thou who hast united opposites!
Rejoice, thou who hast joined virginity and motherhood!
Rejoice, thou through whom sin has been absolved!
Rejoice, thou through whom Paradise is opened!
Rejoice, key to the Kingdom of Christ!

Rejoice, hope of eternal blessings!
Rejoice, unwedded Bride!

KONTAKION 9

All angel kind was amazed at the great act of Thy incarnation; for they saw the inaccessible God as a man accessible to all, dwelling with us and hearing from all: Alleluia!

EIKOS 9

We see most eloquent orators dumb as fish before thee, O Mother of God. For they dare not ask: How canst thou bear a Child and yet remain a Virgin? But we marvel at the mystery, and cry with faith:
Rejoice, receptacle of the Wisdom of God!
Rejoice, treasury of His Providence!
Rejoice, thou who showest philosophers to be fools!
Rejoice, thou who constrainest the learned to silence!
Rejoice, for the clever critics have made fools of themselves!
Rejoice, for the writers of myths have died out!
Rejoice, thou who didst break the webs of the Athenians!
Rejoice, thou who didst fill the nets of the fishermen!
Rejoice, thou who drawest us from the depths of ignorance!
Rejoice, thou who enlightenest many with knowledge!
Rejoice, ship of those who wish to be saved!
Rejoice, haven for sailors on the sea of life!
Rejoice, unwedded Bride!

KONTAKION 10

Wishing to save the world, the Ruler of all came to it spontaneously. And though as God He is our Shepherd, for us He appeared to us as a Man; and having called mankind to salvation by His own Perfect Manhood, as God He hears: Alleluia!

EIKOS 10

Thou art a wall to virgins and to all who run to thee, O Virgin Mother of God. For the Maker of Heaven and earth prepared thee, O Immaculate One, and dwelt in thy womb, and taught all to call to thee:

Rejoice, pillar of virginity!
Rejoice, gate of salvation!
Rejoice, founder of spiritual reformation!
Rejoice, leader of divine goodness!
Rejoice, for thou didst regenerate those conceived in shame!
Rejoice, for thou gavest understanding to those robbed of their senses!
Rejoice, thou who didst foil the corrupter of minds!
Rejoice, thou who gavest birth to the Sower of chastity!
Rejoice, bridechamber of a virgin marriage!
Rejoice, thou who dost wed the faithful to the Lord!
Rejoice, fair mother and nurse of virgins!
Rejoice, betrother of holy souls!
Rejoice, unwedded Bride!

KONTAKION 11

Every hymn falls short that aspires to embrace the multitude of Thy many mercies. For if we should offer to Thee, O Holy King, songs numberless as the sand, we should still have done nothing worthy of what Thou hast given to us who shout to Thee: Alleluia!

EIKOS 11

We see the Holy Virgin as a flaming torch appearing to those in darkness. For having kindled the Immaterial Light, she leads all to divine knowledge; she illumines our minds with radiance and is honoured by our shouting these praises:

Rejoice, ray of the spiritual Sun!

Rejoice, flash of unfading splendour!
Rejoice, lightning that lights up our souls!
Rejoice, thunder that stuns our enemies!
Rejoice, for thou didst cause the refulgent Light to dawn!
Rejoice, for thou didst cause the river of many streams to
  gush forth!
Rejoice, living image of the font!
Rejoice, remover of the stain of sin!
Rejoice, laver that washes the conscience clean!
Rejoice, bowl for mixing the wine of joy!
Rejoice, aroma of the fragrance of Christ!
Rejoice, life of mystical festivity!
Rejoice, unwedded Bride!

KONTAKION 12

When He Who forgives all men their past debts wished to restore us to favour, of His own will He came to dwell among those who had fallen from His grace; and having torn up the record of their sins, He hears from all: Alleluia!

EIKOS 12

While singing to thy Child, we all praise thee as a living temple, O Mother of God. For the Lord Who holds all things in His hand dwelt in thy womb, and He sanctified and glorified thee, and taught all to cry to thee:
Rejoice, tabernacle of God the Word!
Rejoice, saint greater than the saints!
Rejoice, ark made golden by the Spirit!
Rejoice, inexhaustible treasury of Life!
Rejoice, precious diadem of pious kings!
Rejoice, adorable boast of devoted priests!
Rejoice, unshaken tower of the Church!
Rejoice, impregnable wall of the Kingdom!

Rejoice, thou through whom we obtain our victories!
Rejoice, thou before whom our foes fall prostrate!
Rejoice, healing of my body!
Rejoice, salvation of my soul!
Rejoice, unwedded Bride!

KONTAKION 13

O all-praised Mother who didst bear the Word holiest of all the Saints, accept this our offering, and deliver us from all offense, and redeem from future torment those who cry in unison to thee: Alleluia. *(Thrice)*

And again Eikos 1 and Kontakion 1 are read.

PRAYER
to our Most Holy Lady
the Mother of God

My most gracious Queen, my hope, Mother of God, shelter of orphans, and intercessor of travellers, strangers and pilgrims, joy of those in sorrow, protectress of the wronged, see my distress, see my affliction! Help me, for I am helpless. Feed me, for I am a stranger and pilgrim. Thou knowest my offence; forgive and resolve it as thou wilt. For I know no other help but thee, no other intercessor, no gracious consoler but thee, O Mother of God, to guard and protect me throughout the ages. Amen.

The Akathist Icon of the Theotokos, from Koutloumousiou
Monastery on Mount Athos, where the Akathist to the Mother
of God has been sung every day for centuries.

The original Tikhvin Icon of the Mother of God from the
Tikhvin Monastery in the South Ladoga region of Russia, now
treasured in Holy Trinity Cathedral, Chicago.

INDEX

INDEX